Books in the Linkers series

Homes discovered through Art & Technology
Homes discovered through Geography
Homes discovered through History
Homes discovered through Science

Myself discovered through Art & Technology
Myself discovered through Geography
Myself discovered through History
Myself discovered through Science

Toys discovered through Art & Technology
Toys discovered through Geography
Toys discovered through History
Toys discovered through Science

Water discovered through Art & Technology
Water discovered through Geography
Water discovered through History
Water discovered through Science

Food discovered through Art & Technology
Food discovered through Geography
Food discovered through History
Food discovered through Science

Journeys discovered through Art & Technology
Journeys discovered through Geography
Journeys discovered through History
Journeys discovered through Science

First published 1997 A&C Black (Publishers) Limited
35 Bedford Row, London WC1R 4JH

ISBN 0-7136-4778-7
A CIP catalogue record for this book is available from the British Library.

Copyright © 1997 BryantMole Books
Design by Jean Wheeler
Consultant: Hazel Grice

Acknowledgements

Bruce Coleman; J Brakenbury 5 (left), James Davis; 17, Eye Ubiquitous; Darren Maybury 2, Davey Bold 12, A Garrou 15 (bottom), Peter Blake 16 (left), Short Shoot 16 (right), D Gill 19 (right), Skjold 23, Oxford Scientific Films; Michael Leach 3 (right), Nick Bergkessel 5 (right), G I Bernard 7 (below), Hans Reinhard 8 (right), Colin Monteath 22 (left), Positive Images; 10 (left), 13 (top), 22 (right), Tony Stone Images; Art Wolfe 4, Manoj Shah 8 (left), Lori Adamski Peek 11, Christopher Bissell 13 (bottom), Jon Riley 14, Stewart Cohen 15 (top), Pete Seaward 20, Simon McComb 21 (left), Zefa; cover, 3 (left), 6, 7 (top), 9, 10 (right), 18, 19 (left), 21 (right).

Printed and bound in Italy by L.E.G.O.

Journeys

discovered through
Science

Karen Bryant-Mole

Contents

A & C Black • London

Journeys

When something moves from one place to another place, it is making a journey.

Animals

All animals can move.
This means that all animals can make journeys.
The giraffe in this picture had to make a journey to find the leaves it is eating.

Bodies

There are many different ways to move.
Some living things fly.
Others run or jump.
Their bodies allow them to move in some ways and not in others.
This frog can jump and swim but it cannot fly or run.

Machines

Human beings often make journeys in machines.
Cars, buses, vans and motorbikes are some of the machines that we use to make journeys.

This book will help you to discover more about movement, as it explores the science behind journeys.

Through air

Most of the creatures that make journeys through the air, do so by flying.

Birds
This is an eagle.
It is a type of bird.
Birds fly through the air by flapping their wings or by gliding.
Almost all birds can fly but a few, such as the ostrich, can't.

Insects

Many insects can fly.
Like most insects, the grasshopper in the picture below only grew wings when it became an adult.
Some insects have wings that are easy to see.
Others keep their wings folded under wing-cases.

Mammals

A few mammals can move through the air by gliding.
The flying squirrel in the picture above does not have wings to flap.
Instead, it has big pieces of skin between its legs and its body that act like a parachute.

Through water

Many of the animals that move through water, do so by swimming.

Fish
Like most fish, this shark swims by bending first to one side and then the other, making waves down its body.
This makes the shark's tail move from side to side, which pushes it through the water.

Legs
This turtle uses its strong legs to swim.
Toads and frogs use their legs to swim too.

Getting around
There are many other ways to get around in water.
A lobster walks on the sea bed.
An octopus pushes itself through the sea by
squirting out jets of water.
This scallop moves by clapping the two parts of
its shell together.

Over land

Most of the animals that make journeys over land use their legs to walk or run.

Speed

Some animals catch other animals for food. Many meat-eating animals, like the cheetah in the picture below, can run very quickly. Animals that move slowly are often plant-eating animals.
Their food does not run away from them!

Jumping

This kangaroo uses its strong back legs to move by jumping. Other animals that move by jumping include crickets, frogs and rabbits.

Sliding

Some animals have no legs at all.
A snake slithers across the ground.
This snail uses its strong muscly foot to move.
It makes a slimy trail which helps it to slide along.

People

People move from place to place too.

Two legs

Instead of using four or more legs, as most animals do, humans only use two.

As well as walking, we can use our legs to run, jump, climb, hop, skip and even swim.

Joints

Our bodies have a frame inside, called a skeleton.

The skeleton is made up of bones. The places where bones meet are called joints.

Joints in our knees, hips, toes and ankles allow our legs and feet to bend and help us to move easily.

Muscles

There are muscles attached to our bones. They move different parts of our body by pulling the bones. When we want to walk or run, our brain sends messages to muscles in our legs and feet, telling them to work.

Forces

As well as making journeys on foot, we also make journeys in moving vehicles such as cars, planes and boats.

Pushes and pulls

All vehicles need something called a force to make them start moving.
A force is a push or a pull of one type or another.
These children are making a journey in their buggies.
Their mothers make the buggies move by pushing them.

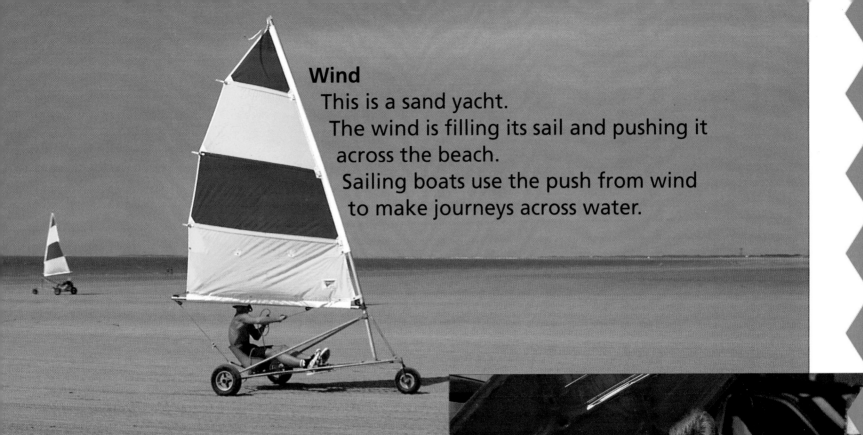

Wind

This is a sand yacht.
The wind is filling its sail and pushing it across the beach.
Sailing boats use the push from wind to make journeys across water.

Engines

Many journeys are made in vehicles that get their push from an engine.
This car has an engine.
Can you think of any other vehicles that have engines?

Engines

Most road vehicles use a type of engine called an internal combustion engine.

Fuel

An engine needs fuel to make it work.
A fuel is anything that burns.
Most cars use either petrol or diesel as their fuel.

Internal combustion engines work by making a series of tiny explosions.
The explosions are made when air and fuel are mixed together and lit by a spark.

Wheels

Each explosion pushes a piece inside the engine downwards.

This pushing is used to turn other parts in the engine that are linked to the car's wheels.

They make the wheels turn and allow the car to move.

Jet engines

Most planes have jet engines.

Jet engines suck air in and then push it out very quickly. This pushes the plane through the air.

Getting faster

When we make journeys, we move at different speeds.

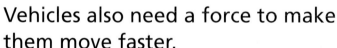

Forces

Once something is moving, it carries on moving at the same speed unless a force works on it.
To make something move faster requires more push or pull.
To run faster, the athletes on the right push harder with their legs.

Vehicles

Vehicles also need a force to make them move faster.
A car travels faster when its engine works harder.
The harder the car's engine works, the more fuel it uses.
A bike travels faster when its rider pushes down harder on the pedals.

Downhill
These sledges speed up when they travel downhill.
This is because of a force called gravity.
Gravity is a special force that pulls things downwards.
When you throw a ball into the air, it is gravity that pulls it back down to the ground.

Slowing down

Moving things slow down because of a force called friction.

Friction
Friction happens whenever two things rub together.

The tyres on this lorry are rubbing against the road.
If the lorry's engine stopped working, the rubbing would make the lorry slow down.
Eventually it would stop.

Brakes

Many vehicles are fitted with brakes.
Bike brakes work by making brake pads
squeeze against the wheels.
This creates a lot of friction and slows the
bike down very quickly. *quite*
The brake pads are connected to levers on
the handlebars by wires.

Uphill

Travelling uphill makes
things slow down too.
This is because gravity is
trying to pull them
downwards.
This runner has to work
much harder to run up
a hill than he does to run
on flat ground.

19

Changing direction

Forces

The driver of this lorry needs to make his lorry change direction, so that it can go round bends in the road. To make something change direction you need to make forces work on it. This means that it needs pushes or pulls of one type or another.

Controlling the direction of something is called steering.

Turning

When this cyclist wants to make a turn, he pulls one handlebar towards him and pushes one handlebar away from him.
This twists the front wheel and makes the bike change direction.

Steering

The sailor in the picture above is steering his boat using a ship's wheel. The wheel is connected to a rudder in the water. When the rudder is moved the boat changes direction.
Bikes are steered with handlebars.
Cars and buses have steering wheels.

Energy

Energy is what makes things go or work. Everything that makes journeys needs a source of energy.

Animals

Animals get their energy from food.
The camel in the picture below can store up energy inside its humps by eating lots of food.
Most animals, including people, cannot store up energy like this.
We have to eat regular meals.

Vehicles

This tram uses electricity from overhead wires as its source of energy.
Cars use petrol or diesel.
Planes use aviation fuel.
A bicycle's rider is its source of energy.

Using energy

As we move from place to place we use energy.

The more difficult the journey, the more energy we use.

This jogger is using more energy than she would be if she was walking.

The next time you make a journey, think about the source of energy being used.

Glossary

gliding flying on warm, rising air, without flapping wings
insect an animal with six legs
levers bars which can be lifted or pressed to make things move
mammals animals with warm blood, which feed their young with milk
muscles bundles of thin bands that move parts of the body
regular at set times
rudder a flat piece of wood or metal on a boat, used for steering
spark a tiny bit of fire

Index

How to use this book

Each book in this series takes a familiar topic or theme and focuses on one area of the curriculum: science, art and technology, geography or history. The books are intended as starting points, illustrating some of the many different angles from which a topic can be studied. They should act as springboards for further investigation, activity or information seeking.

Science
- journeys involve movement
- all animals can make journeys
- animals can move in different ways
- joints and muscles allow movement
- journeys can be made in vehicles
- many vehicles have engines
- forces make things move
- forces make things speed up and slow down
- forces make things change direction
- energy is needed to make things go

Art and Technology
- roads and vehicles have to be designed
- journeys feature in works of art
- design road signs
- make a wheeled toy vehicle
- investigate flexible ways of joining
- make a toy boat that can move
- test paper gliders
- design an imaginary vehicle
- draw a picture map
- create a 'journey' game

JOURNEYS
key concepts and activities explored within each book

History
changes have taken place during the past one hundred years, relating to:
- the way vehicles are powered
- the uses of vehicles
- the design of vehicles
- the number of car owners
- the design of roads
- the work of people who make journeys possible
- journeys across water and through the air
- journeys to work and journeys on holiday

Geography
- the frequency and distance of journeys can vary
- there are a variety of methods of transport
- there is a difference between public and private transport
- journeys have beginnings and endings
- many people help to make journeys possible
- animals and goods, as well as people, make journeys
- maps are useful when making journeys
- journeys have an impact on the environment